AN ODE OF A 10 YEAR OLD

TANEESHA OMER

AURAQ
PUBLICATIONS

Printed in the Islamic Republic of Pakistan.

Printed: April, 2022
Edition: 1st
ISBN: 978-969-749-170-4
Price: Rs 999 PKR, $10 US

www.auraqpublications.com | raabta@auraqpublications.com
@AuraqPublications | @AuraqBooks | +92-300-0571-530
Printed and Bound by *Passive Printers* - www.passiveprinters.com

DEDICATIONS

I would like to dedicate this book to my
encouraging, beautiful family-

Omer Farooq, Zoona Saeed, Ahmed Omer and
Wareesha Omer

ACKNOWLEDGEMENTS

First of all, I would like to appreciate my parents, Zoona Saeed and Omer Farooq for helping me throughout my book writing journey and giving me encouragement when I needed it the most. I am also very grateful to my brother, Ahmed Omer, for being an inspiration as he instilled a thought of being a young author by exemplifying himself. My wholesome gratitude to my grandparents – Neelam Farooq, Muhammad Saeed and Roohi Saeed for giving me bucketloads of support and encouragement. The contribution made by Mrs Humaira Arshad for enhancing my poetry skills, is well acknowledged.

I wish the book was published when my dearest great grandmother (Late) Jamila Malik was physically with us but I know she would be super proud of me, smiling in heavens as she was a star who had always enlightened us with her vast knowledge and cherished our efforts and successes.

CONTENTS

Who am I?

With a brother named Ahmed and a sister named Wareesha

Here I am standing in the spotlight Taneesha

You know who I am, I am the author of this book

So let's open it now and get the first look

I love who I am

My life is full of glam

Now I'll share a few fun facts about me

I really do love swimming in the sea

Those who know, me who I am

Know that I dislike the language of slang

My parents help me all day and night

Zoona and Omer, you heard that right

As a family we cherish our lives

And live together like bees in a hive

So that's all from my side

Let's read the book and take a big stride

What is the most important thing in life?

What is the most important thing in life

Is it family, love, or to be organized?

Well, out of all these great things

It will give your mind a big ting

As it is to have gratitude

To give respect and not be rude

No one can take this away from you

And you can develop good habits too

We have to be patient and kind

And keep our thoughts to our mind

Then good things will happen in life

Without getting scared or having a fright

You will also get a lot of applause

And that is just because

You achieved the most important thing in life

And now everyone can see your bright shining light

COVID-19

We have to wear a mask

And that is quite a hard task

We have to be careful

So that we are less tearful

Everyone has to do his or her part

Whether it is easy or hard

We have to stay inside

To stay healthy and alive

We can fight this off together

And stay in peace forever

Vaccination is the only cure

And doctors are saying that, for sure

We need to prevent COVID-19

No matter if we are young, old or in our teens

So don't pretend to be ignorant

Help those whose lives are stagnant

Summer holidays

We are all waiting

For the school bell to ring

Everyone is excited

And I am delighted

We suddenly heard the bell

And all of us gave a yell

We said our final goodbyes

And my class teacher started to cry

We all hugged each other

And gave gifts to one another

Our three long months had now started

And to our homes we all darted

The vacations were from June fifth

And lasted till September sixth

The land of Pakistan

Declared independence on August 14, 1947

For Muslims at that time it was Heaven

They were all very delighted

As Pakistan was being sighted

AIlam-a-Iqbal envisaged our land

Quaid-a-Azam delivered it with a fool proof plan

They fought a big rival

For our peace and survival

Many people sadly passed away

And slept on cold beds made of hay

Now we live in this beautiful place

And work together to make it safe

We should have a lot of pride

And take tests in our stride

So how about all of us give a true salute

To the ones who saved us from long abuse

The Needy

Have you ever walked in a town

That made you raise a frown

Do you ever see people who are dirty

And felt the need to be guilty

Have you ever seen any of those

People without water and clothes?

Please just stop and think

Before these poor people sink

Some people are ill on the street

While you enjoy your tender-cooked meat

While you sleep on your bed

They may have never been fed

So how about for once you stop by

And give them a meal or a shoulder to cry?

Help them fulfil their needs

For once in a while, at least

Let's change the sadness and frowns

All upside down

My sweet Mother

My Mother does work sitting on her chair

She is sweet, loving and always cares

She constantly likes to share

Even though sometimes I act like a bear

She encourages me all along

And corrects me nicely if I am wrong

She definitely is really sweet

From time to time she gives me a surprise treat

She is very very smart

And always has things In her online cart

She likes to plays fun games with me

And gets very scared when something approaches
like a bee

Her favourite colour is red

And she has repeatedly said

"You are the best, East or West

This is the one bit that I readily accept"

My Favourite things

Trees full of blossoms and Harry Potter

Family together and people who matter

Soft woollen pillows loosened by tapping

These are a few of my favourite things

Babies that giggle and for goodness sake

Some lampshades and delicious cake

Online quizzes that go ting ting ting

These are a few of my favourite things

Spaghetti and Meatballs and Urdu lessons

Playing with family table tennis-sessions

The old fashioned telephone that always rings

These are a few of my favourite things

When the Ink dries out

When children are loud

When I am sad

I simply remember my favourite things

And then don't feel so bad

Save the world

Have you seen the pollution

And have you ever thought about the solution?

How can we not take action

When there is so much destruction?

We have to save the earth

As it has a lot of worth

It's so delicate when you think

It could easily vanish in a blink

Take a look around in your town

You will be disgusted and surely frown

Smog seems to be the order of the day

The chances of a bright future are withering away

Environmental pollution is destroying our lives

We better wake up as time flies

How about all of us save the Earth

From this treacherous curse

Family

These people are with you for your whole life

They may be children, a husband or a good wife

No one should underestimate a family

As being with them makes it heavenly

A Brother, A sister, A mom and A dad

Are enough people to prevent you from being sad

They teach valuable lessons every day

And every year celebrate your Birthday

They care for you with all their hearts

Right from the very start

They make sure you get the best

And when you need it they let you rest

Whenever you are sick or have a flu

They always are there for you

So let's respect our dear ones

And enjoy our lives with everyone

Oh! It's a wonderful World

Eating lollipops with swirls

When my hair has curls

The stars are shining so bright

Like the yellow fireflies

Oh! It's a wonderful world

Playing with my family

And watching little Timithy

Going in the swimming pool

And when the weather is cool

Oh! It's a wonderful world

When I am watching the sunset

When the ball is stuck in the net

Eating yummy nuts

And Ice-cream trucks

Oh! It's a wonderful world

NewMonong (Nonsense Verse)

In all the myths and fairy tales

There was a caution sign and beware

For who would fight the NewMonong

A breed of a Lion, Lizard and Hong

Then on a very rainy day

A prince wanted the NewMonong to be slayed

The Nemonong started to say "Berry Lerry"

And the prince became very merry

The NewMonong put up a fight

And was slain at the dawn of night

They all said jibber rib fib

And bragged about this as long as they lived

People (Nonsense Verse)

The people cooked their meals

And even added steel

One added a hint of Bing Bong

While the other choked on Ting Tong

The pots went Bib Bab Bob

Then came in some hobs

These tiny fairies

Were quite scary

They cast a spell

And everyone started to tell

The most embarrassing Truths

And one even ate a moose!

My Father

My father is the best

From all of the rest

He cares for us all the time

And makes us feel divine

He teaches us life learning lessons every day

And he always does that in the best way

He makes me giggle all the time

And whenever I am with him I always shine

He helps us when we have a problem

And makes us feel happy when we are solemn

He does the best for everyone

And has never hurt anyone

Although he is very sweet and kind

He still actually has a brilliant and intelligent mind

I love my father from the core of my heart

And he has done so from the very start

My little mad sister

My little sister is very lazy

And normally behaves very crazy

She pulls my hair

And never shares

She gets up at midnight

To pick up a fight

She's a very picky eater

And pretends she's the best leader

She throws things all the time

And never asks, "Are you fine?"

She sometimes makes me mad

And then herself pretends to be sad

She is one of a kind

And has a very diligent mind

She gives me a kiss and a hug

And shares her milk in a mug

She does annoy me from time to time

But her laughter always helps me shine

We do get along

And sing many songs

Even though she's so cheeky

And to make her behave is really tricky

I love her from head to toe

And also hope she does so

Doctors

If you are terribly sick

A doctor would help you get fit

Doctors save our lives

And help people survive

Sure they have needles

But they give it so we don't become feeble

If there were no doctors during the pandemic

The consequences could have been worse than tragic

Their job is magical

And prevents Covid becoming lethal

They are risking their own lives

For the betterment of human kind

We need to admire their work

As a token towards what they deserve

It's a pity so many have lost their lives

While keeping their oath to continue the fight

One day I dream to be like them

And help humanity till the very end

Honesty

Have you ever told a lie

And felt guilty about it for your whole life?

That's when honesty comes in place

And if you are honest you will be amazed

People will believe you more

As you have now tore

The worst habit of lying

Into telling the truth and flying

You can develop the best habits to

From just telling the truth

You will also feel the change

And get lots of fame

So let's all show honesty

As it's the best policy

The Rich

The Rich have a dream life

Compared to the ones who lag in stride

Many want to have that much money

And say they would give away anything like being funny

But how is it to live the rich life

And is it really as amazing as we sight

Well let's take a look at it

And see every detail that we missed

First are they really happy

And do they have a loving caring family

Second are they kind

And have a diligent mind

Lastly do they have true friends

To stick with them to the end

That's what matters in life

Not if you look good at first sight

So let's all be grateful

And never again be hateful

To those who care for us

And stood tall when we made a fuss

The future

As I started to daydream in school

I saw something very cool

It was the future

And how robots almost took over

They did everything for us

And were making no sort of fuss

They looked after everyone

And could gain the trust of anyone

They were as fast as the speed of light

And would stop any war, conflict or fight

They helped anyone in need

And everyday would plant a tree

Though the humans were now pretty lazy

And some even went crazy

Most of them practiced sports

For half an hour or sometimes even more

So the future isn't looking that bad

Though it does drive some people mad

At the Break of Dawn

In the soil many flowers reside

Swaying from side to side

The birds chirp melodious tunes

And the sun will rise soon

There is a light breeze

It is only seven degrees

The animals slowly walk

While the humans calmly talk

There is a soft sprinkle of rain

But no one can see it through the window pane

Many are having a short jog

In the disappearing fog

The sky is a soft blue

To match a beautiful dew

When the sun reaches its centre stage

The beauties of dawn start to fade

Too Many cooks are in the shop

All of the cooks are starting to fight

As they want to prove their individual might

Everyone has a different taste

But some are only getting others' waste

They are fighting over the grilled potatoes

And stealing the others' freshly picked tomatoes

Some need only a few fruit

While others need the vegetables to

They are all running like crazy ants

And are all starting to pant

Some are sprinting to the cash register

While others are rushing for the remaining lady-fingers

Some have finally left the store

But in come a lot more

Stars

Shining bright at night

And showing an amazing light

They are made out of gas

But never explode that fast

Twinkling in the sky

They remain very high

These things are stars

And from Earth they are very far

While they float in space

They leave a beautiful trace

They are everywhere in the galaxy

But are too far from humanity

The Sun is even a star

And it is always glowing hard

People love stars truly

Because of all their beauty

I really love stars

And always stare at them from afar

A lady from Lorne (Limerick)

A lovely young lady from Lorne

Wakes up with the sound of a ships horn

She lives by the seaside

Though in Math she doesn't know how to divide
(cut it out)

She loves seawater and fresh popped corn

Cow Show (Limerick)

There is an old cow at the show

Who is portly and possesses a bow

He is exceedingly obnoxious

To poor cats he is monstrous

And he lives in a make belief place called Mow

A dog (Limerick)

There once was a dog from Kowloon

Who always had a cute yellow balloon

He had ombrophobia

Though he sat in a cage with claustrophobia

And he never slept till Noon!

Pete (Limerick)

There once was a fellow called Pete

He always dropped dictionaries on his feet

Pete always used to fight

With the fireflies at night

He never liked to sit on seats

Hypocrisy

Have you ever exaggerated what you said

Posed it at a level you never met

It's something called 'hypocrisy'

And for us humans we take it easy

Helping one but saying you helped nine

Making up things crosses the red line

Now that is called Hypocrisy

And getting away with it might be stress-free

Hypocrisy might seem like a small issue

But we can't wipe it away like it's a tissue

As they say honesty

Is the best policy

So stick to what you have actually done

And don't make up things just for fun

We all have to support each other

So we end this, one way or another

Zoo

As we hear the lion's roar

In the sky the birds soar

Even though the lion is caged

Still it gets the children engaged

This is called the Zoo

And there are many more animals to

Like the giraffes so high

That there almost touching the sky

And the fish in the pond

Which make a spilsh splash song

Look! There is an elephant

Walking in great elegance

Vendors are selling Ice cream

Beside the bear team

I love the Zoo

And I hope you do too!

The road to success

With hard work always comes the best

But with laziness you will be far behind from the rest

Sure the first step is always the hardest

You'll achieve your goals, the fastest

Skipping steps might seem easy at first

But later on you'll feel like you're cursed

But if you take the steps one-by-one

You can get recognized by anyone

You'll also feel very glad and great

As in front of you you'll have the best fate

But if you skip steps you will soon realize

Your future is filled with cries

Now if you follow all of the steps

You'll be on the road to success

The Seasons

The four seasons are

Autumn, spring, summer and winter as the last

In spring it's always perfect to

Ride a bike and jump in the pool

While in winter it's freezing cold

So we have to stay inside as we are told

In summer it's burning hot

Much more than as we initially thought

In autumn all the leaves fall

But it's never ugly not at all

In winter the animals hibernate

So they don't have the cold to face

I love spring with all my heart

As it has a beautiful start

So I love all the seasons

For their separate reasons

Foxes

As it becomes the dark night

A creature howls and in comes a shiver of fright

With fur as soft as a baby's skin

It rummages through in a litterbin

Living in the woods and hunting mice

It never gets a bit of fright

This creature is the sly fox

Though it can be as strong as an ox

It does come in many species

And have excellent hunting abilities

Foxes are really great

And their cubs are adorable when they mate

Sensing their really big orange ears

They run away if trouble is near

That's why foxes are the best

From the animal kingdom and the rest

Roses

Walking around the garden I see

A beautiful little bumblebee

Though what could it be sitting on

That's taking it oh so long

It's a beautiful soft shiny red rose

And it showers every day with the hose

Roses aren't just red

They have a very velvety head

Their fragrance is from out of this world

And they are as shiny as pearls

Roses are much better than perfume

As they freshen up a whole room

Roses are the most beautiful things

As they bloom in Spring

Roses have a very warm place in my heart

Ever since I saw one from the very start

Winter has arrived

The dreaded winter has come

To suck up all the fun

We can't go outdoors

And inside we get bored

You can easily get a fever

So everything has to be cleaner

The animals hibernate

So they don't have the icy cold to face

Rain is pouring all the time

And everyone is starting to whine

No outdoor sports can be played

And we only have video games

We have to wear itchy high necks

And multiple layers of vests

Though this is only what I ponder

Your might have a different wonder

2020

The worst year let's talk about that

While putting on our new year's hat

First these major bush fires

Making the forest even more drier

Cancer also increased a lot

Though the people tried and they fought

Though the worst thing about this year

And what we all greatly fear

Is this Covid-19

Which none of us had ever seen

We all had to wear a mask

And that wasn't the easiest task

We stayed away from our family

Which made our heart really heavy

That's why 2020 is the worst year

And let's hope 2021 will bring some cheer

White

The colour that is the most pure

And that it is, for sure

This is the majestic white

Shining in the moonlight

It has a lot of positive meanings

Which stops us from grieving

White also makes us calm

And stops the anger alarm

After looking at it you'll feel at ease

As white is just so good to please

It can also show cleanliness

And even symbolize friendliness

I really love the colour white

Since it shines so bright

White is my favourite colour

Is yours the same or another

Autumn has come

As the tree leaves start to fall

Which is not ugly, not at all

We know autumn has arrived

As our skin is getting dried

We can jump into a pile of leaves

As they're falling off the trees

You can bake a yummy pie

And make your pumpkin DIY

We can get loads of candy

And be super happy

We can wear our Halloween costumes

Or see the sunflowers bloom

You can host a board game night

And everyone gets excited at first sight

Even though the animals wake up late

Autumn is really great

Summers here

As we start to sweat

We take a shower to get wet

Summer has arrived

And we have all realized

So let's see what to do

And it there's anything new

First we can dive into the pool

Be relaxed and become cool

Wear half sleeve T-shirts

And observe busy little creatures

We have drinks with Ice

As there's a lot of sunlight

We have a great mood

And eat a lot of healthy food

Summer is so much fun

Especially due to the sun

Doves

What is this bird that is white

And nests with its eggs at night

It's of course the beautiful dove

That soars way above

Doves are also really smart

And their love is as strong as a human's heart

Doves fly fifty miles per hour

And eat the seeds of a variety of flowers

They normally lay their eggs from April to July

Once the eggs hatch the mother starts to fly

Their babies are very cute

But in the first few weeks their mom gets them food

Spotting doves is very easy

And they look extremely pretty

So if you ever buy a bird

In my case doves are preferred

My new school

As I packed my school bag

I felt nervous, excited and sad

For I was going to a new school

Would it be boring or super cool

I stood by the school gate

For what would be my fate?

I took a deep breath

And inside I stepped

I was taken to my class

My introduction was a bit fast

Everyone was really nice

And I felt no fright

The teachers were also welcoming

And everyone started helping

Now I've been at LGS for 4 years

And have never felt a bit of fear

The Weeping Willow

Once a long time ago

Wept a willow all alone

The birds had gone afar

Leaving a single lark

The leaves had broken down

A shiver of fear all around

Whoever would touch this tree

Would never again be seen

Not even the smartest detective

Could find out the location of the captives

It was once a beautiful blossom

Repelling anything rotten

Yet one fine day autumn came

And things were never the same

As it watched its beauty fall down

And other trees take the prettiness crown

The tree sought revenge

From those who had made its happiness end

Little did it know this hidden foe

Was mother nature with a seasonal blow

It thought its demise was due to the nearby
community

And now it was releasing its anger in all its fury

48

My Big Brother

I saw you when I was just born

You have guided me for so long

You have no idea how proud I am

Without you I won't be able to stand

You have given me a lot of care

And with me you are always fair

You help me all the time

And you're super kind

Whenever I am about to fall

You help me stand towering tall

You tell me off from time to time

But it's only for my benefit, and I don't mind

You coach me in many games

Which will lead me to my fame

You always help me improve

Whether it's big or a small move

You are always there when I need you the most

To help me accomplish my dreams and goals

You have written a wonderful book

That gets the readers hooked

You have the pure heat of a dove

And the nine brains of an octopus

You laugh, you giggle, you smile

For your family you would run a 100 miles

I feel like the luckiest girl

As you're the best brother in the world

Night (Horror Poem)

When the moon shines

A shiver runs down our spine

For the wolves attack their midnight feast

And the boys hide under their bedsheets

I see dots on the silver moon

As the birds flap some melodious tunes

Flying away from the deadly trees

In my vision their running away from bees

Tears fill my eyes

"I ask for forgiveness for that day's lies"

I look away from the window

Filled with loads of sorrow

I then see my bed

And doze on it like I am dead

War is not an option

War is a global problem

That has made many people solemn

War makes people tremendously sad

People sadly perishing and world leaders mad

But on the other hand think of a world with peace

Cheerfulness and enjoyment would significantly increase

The atrocities of war have a great impact

War is gruesome and that's a fact

Why make people weep and cry

Why betray our closest allies

Why not live with each other happily

Why arm guns and shoot each other sadly

How many nuclear bombs do we have to use

How many missiles do we have to fuse

Let's try to live in a happy world

All I want to say is take my word

I know I am young I know I am ten

I know that than me there are many stronger women and men

But I will make an immense impact

I'll grow up to be very compact

I'll try to spread global peace

And put all these wars to a cease

Darkness (Horror)

It does get lonely up here

I must say I must fear

While they can play and play

I am stuck here all day

They said they would come at five

Petrified but thankfully alive

Darkness surrounds me everywhere

Banging, Crashing and Nightmares

I am different from everyone else

My skin, religion and what else

I am lucky if the yells don't come

Chomping away what is left of fun

Sometimes I try to sit and think

What causes me from joy to misery in a blink

Instead of counting lovely sheep

I see people and hear bloody screams

Witches possess my heart and soul

Killing the only innocent foul

Sometimes I see ghostly spirits

Maliciously singing nursery rhyme lyrics

Not the lovely ones we sing to our children

But the ones which will curse and are forbidden

I start to tear up

But they enjoy drinking them in a cup

I am always pinned against the wall

Though never weak enough to fall

My head spins like the wheel of a cycle

The sweet children I knew suddenly become psycho's

I feel like a disappoint as it's my fate

I look at the clock it's too late

I am a part of darkness now

Run away, go screaming to the town

I don't want to hurt anyone else

So I have started to cut myself

I have only felt happiness once or twice

And both have given me immense fright

Happy endings will never exist

Otherwise it would have been number one on my wish list

I cannot experience this again

So I think this may be then end....

Animal Cruelty

I am stuck in this small jail

As according to my owner I have failed

I do not have the best tricks any more

And now I am considered at best, as a "bore"

My owners don't want me to sleep anymore

Because I have recently started to snore

They hit and pull my long ears

Giving me greater freights and fears

One time stones were thrown at my eye

Though my owner threatened me if I cried

That really hurt and made me half blind

I had to limp as they injured my hinds

My food was costed as way too high

While they ate expensive turkey with delight

Though one day with my vision blurry

I saw a kind woman who was in a hurry

My tail started to wag with joy

Would I finally be out of this prison and not be
treated like a toy

To my joy the answer was yes

I am feeling better and making progress

The people actually care for me now

For me to go outside, they actually allow

With a relief, I can now proudly say

I am loved again and the past were my bad days

Spring has sprung

Spring has finally sprung

And fresh air has stars to fill in our lungs

Here are the butterflies

The bird's are flying in the skies

So many melodious tunes

And I can't smell any toxic fumes

The bees are surrounding the beautiful flowers

After they take a quick water shower

I see such magnificent trees

Which have so many fresh, green leaves

The time has come

To finally play in the sun

Everyone is delighted

As Spring is being sighted

Printed and Bound by *Passive Printers* - www.passiveprinters.com
Printing press that offers Print on Demand (POD) Facility.
Printed in The Islamic Republic of Pakistan.